BE GOOD TO GOD'S MONEY

And Your Money Will Be Good To You!

BE GOOD TO GOD'S MONEY

And Your Money Will Be Good To You!

LISA FRYE

L L Q PUBLISHING COMPANY

L L Q Publishing Company
631 N. Stephanie Street
Suite 311
Henderson, NV 89014

Printed in the United States of America

Library of Congress Control Number: 2006907412

Cover design by: Innovative Images

ISBN-10: 0-9726032-0-4
ISBN-13: 978-0-972603-20-1

This book is dedicated to the source of my every being, a Power greater than myself, and greater than I could ever image. The Angels that guided my steps, when I had and didn't have money.

CONTENTS

INTRODUCTION

Living below your means" is a phrase that has been associated with poverty. Many motivational speakers consider it "poverty thinking". Let's take a look at what living below your means, really means. If your annual income is $10 million, then living below your means could mean living off of $5 million, annually. Considering where many of us have been, $5 million is not a bad "below the means". The famed billionaires Oprah Winfrey, Bill Gates, the late Sam Walton, and Warren Buffett continuously comment on how they live below their means. I don't know about you, but I feel like this is the class to be in, if living below your means can create the billionaire in me.

It doesn't mean that you should not have nice things or that you don't deserve them. It simply means don't become "a servant to your things".

There is a saying: "Some people spend money they don't have, to buy things they don't need, to impress people they don't like". This is all too common, in the church, in more ways than one.

Don't let material pursuits cause you to live a life of deceit and pretense. We need to keep in mind another modern-day proverb: "It is good to have money and the things that money will buy, but it's also good to make sure you haven't lost the things that money "can't buy".

Did you know that God had more to say about the stewardship of money, than any other subject, in the Bible? The Bible has over 2000 verses that deal with money, finances, and financial planning. Some of those verses deal with topics such as budgets, debt, financial planning, savings, investing, tithing, and much more. The book of Proverbs, a guidebook with wise advice on numerous subject, contains financial guidance to help us manage money wisely. He focused on this subject so often, because He knew how easily we can let money become an idol to us. If we are not careful, it can become the "true" Lord of our lives.

Money can be an integral part of the right kind of success. Some say money is a necessary evil. It is certainly a necessary medium of exchange, but it doesn't have to be evil. Whether money is a good or bad influence, depends on our approach to it. Jesus Christ wasn't opposed to wealth or a high standard of living. The Bible states He became poor, so we could become rich. He simply does not want us to lift money to idol status. The Bible directs us toward the abundant life He wants us to enjoy.

Christian money management is crucial to a believer's financial stewardship. On the other hand, the love of money has corrupted and twisted the lives of many Christians and is a root cause of much evil. No matter how much or how little money we have, if we are not careful, it can become one of the greatest sources of stress in our lives. In fact, money can bring more pain than pleasure! We must not let money become overly important to us.

It is essential we return a portion of what we receive, to the One who gave it. Acknowledging and giving to the One who owns all, who shares with us what we need to survive and prosper, helps us keep physical things in their proper perspective.

We can and ought to be enjoying Christian

finances-- finances that have God in them. And yet, like everything we have available from God, it can be there for you, but you can be missing out totally on the experience of it.

For this reason, I am sharing with you, the message God has given me. After assessing the Spirit of Wealth, God has blessed me tremendously! Giving of my time, my talents, and my money is my way of saying "Thank you". I have tasted "freedom" and "bondage", and freedom tastes better. Be blessed!

Proverbs 22:7 (KJV): "The rich ruleth over the poor, and the borrower is servant to the lender".

DEBT

Do you find it amazing that so many Christians, in the body of Christ, are experiencing financial hardship? Our Father, owns everything, yet we are suffering financially, daily. The blood of Jesus has redeemed us from the curse so that the blessings of Abraham may come on us through Him. But, are we in position to receive our blessings?

Financially, we are positioned in Christ to experience our lives set in the sphere of heavenly economics. We can expect to be shielded from the uncertainties and unreliability of this world's economic. Yet, we block our blessings with mountains of debt.

Money makes a good servant but a poor master. It can separate us from our families and God, if we find ourselves caught up in an unsinkable race for more possessions. Wealth can intoxicate and enslave us. The Apostle Paul spoke of learning to be content with and enjoy the things we have.

As Christians we must learn to be content with what we can afford. We need to recognize the difference between what we need to survive and the luxuries that surround us. We need to learn a new concept -- if we can not afford it -- do without it. We must began to ask ourselves, do we have enough to eat? Do we have a place to live? Do we have clothes to wear? These are the necessities. We should not purchase more things unless we can afford them. We are to be satisfied with our daily necessities until we are out of debt and *stop* creating more debt beyond our capacity of paying.

I have done seminars across the country, in both churches and the public sector. I have noticed that the church members have more debt than the world. I have been in the church all of my life, yet over the past 15 years, I have noticed members coming to church with new outfits every Sunday. I'm sure each of you have been to a church, where there is a "sister" that wears a different outfit all 52 Sundays of the year. Many of you belong to a church where there are two or three "sisters", who are trying to outdress the Pastor's wife. In getting to know some of these women, I have found they have a *tremendous* amount of debt. They look good. They appear to be doing good, however there lives are in complete shambles. They have no peace. Their marriages and families are in total chaos. Their debt is beyond their ability to pay, within the next 40 to 50 years. But, they come to church every Sunday, with the look of success. Many of them are taking the outfits back to the store, on Monday mornings, because they can't afford them.

Debt is a thief. It robs us of our time and money. When we'll working two and three jobs, we do not have time to spend with our family. Debt causes worry and anxiety, which leads to high medical bills and frequent hospital visits. Debt causes conflict with family members and friends. There are so many families that are broken because of money owed to another. Family members no longer speak or attend family functions because of debt issues. The number one cause of divorce is money. The family, usually, have a truckload of debt, causing arguments over money. Debt destroys our Christian witness. It prevents us from being a blessing to God and others around us. In too many cases, we are captured by the stronghold of debt, for a whole lifetime, without even realizing it.

A person will never be able to become totally free, financially, if he or she cannot control spending. Debt is much more than monthly payments. People can fall into a spirit of debt. When debt gets out of control, it can render you useless to the kingdom of God. It becomes your master. It can weaken the basic foundation of the average family and is usually accompanied by improper financial planning or no planning at all.

It has been said that the test of a man's character is how he spends his time and money. When we do not pay our bills on time, we are lying and stealing. Christians are to pay what they owe. According to Romans 13: 8: "Owe no man anything, but to love one another: for he that loveth another hath fulfilled the law". Owe no man anything. It does not mean do not borrow money or buy on credit. What this means is pay your bills (or your balances) when they are due, and do not commit yourself to more than you can afford.

Overspending can result in financial bondage as well as a lack of money. This is not the godly way to run finances. It goes without saying that we need money to live and meet the basic needs. The Bible teaches that true financial freedom requires that we become good stewards. With discipline and help from the Holy Spirit, this is possible. Remember, a good plan will require control as well as action. Although a budget may require sacrifice on our part, it can lead to freedom.

Exercising patience is critical to breaking the stronghold of debt. The Bible encourages us to seek wisdom and counsel, for our financial situations. It is sometimes a challenge to find an ethical financial advisor. Therefore as Christians, we must seek God before we seek counsel. The simple truth is that the greatest difference between wealthy individuals and those who do not achieve wealth, is the advice of their counselors. Not only do they seek the advice, but they follow it. They know that wealth comes with obedience. We must learn how to bring ourselves back to God's will and become obedient.

Luke 15: 13-14 (KJV): "And not many days after the younger son gathered all together, and took his journey into a far country, and there wasted his substance with riotous living. And when he had spent all, there arose a mighty famine in that land; and he began to be in want".

WASTE

As you turn this page, I am sure you expected to find a chapter on budgeting, saving, and financial planning. I did not include a chapter on financial planning, budgeting, savings because you already know what do. You have probably read every financial book that's for sale, including my national bestseller, Be Good To Your Money . I don't need to tell you about your finances and how to get them under control. If you have not done anything about your finances, it is because you want to continue to live the life you are living. You have decided it is better to keep up with the Jones, than be in God's will. So, the next chapter is for those who have chosen to do the right thing. This chapter is for the Christians who have begun to remove the debt or have removed the debt, so they can inherent God's financial blessings for themselves, their children, and their children's children.

Hosea 4:6 says "My people are destroyed for lack of knowledge". This is true, but it is not true concerning finances. I feel it is safe to say, that 95% of Christians know exactly what to do financially. It is not a lack of knowledge that is causing lack. It is our greed, disobedience, and selfishness, that has caused us to be financially dead.

Many Christians can probably quote 10 scriptures from the Bible that explains the riches we are to receive. There are many Christians who can flip back and forth in their Bible and find verses which talk about money, prosperity, and our inheritance from God. Yet, we continue to spend beyond our means. We continue to not pay our debts. We continue to make promises that we know we are not capable of keeping. We continue to write "bad" checks to the church and others. So, it is not a lack of knowledge that is destroying us financially, it is our constant desire to **not** do the right thing.

We have allowed satan to control our lives and our finances. Knowledge, understanding, and doing the right thing goes hand in hand. To have the knowledge and understanding, and not do the right thing is useless.

In Genesis, God promises Abraham (?) that he would inherit the earth and everything within it. In line with inheritance, everything I have is left to my children. If I have nothing, they receive nothing. If I have much, they receive much. If I have the earth and everything within it, they receive the earth and everything within it. Do you feel like you have received the earth and everything within it? Or do you feel like you have just a nibble of your block or neighborhood? Or do you feel like you own a "piece of the rock"?

Proverbs 13: 22 (KJV): "A good man leaveth an inheritance to his children's children: and the wealth of the sinner is laid up for the just".

INHERITANCE

Where is the inheritance that God has promised you? Have you wasted it with undisciplined living and ungodly habits? Are you giving it back to creditor for mountains of debt? Are you allowing your children to waste it away, while trying to make sure they have more than what you had? Did you give it away with your negative thoughts and talk? Have you gambled it away? Did you lose it in a get-rich-quick-scheme? Again, I ask--where is your inheritance?

Financial success includes controlling selfish desires. We want everything yesterday or now. It is important to control our wants. Once you earn money, you must manage it properly. Otherwise, it will soon be gone, with little to show for it. There is an old saying, "A fool and his money will soon part".

Some Christians seem to perpetually have holes in their pockets. Their money go out as fast as it come in. They just can't seem to hang onto what they earn (their inheritance).

Many Christians have prayed prayer on top of prayer, for years, asking God to bless them with more money. We have even memorized *The Prayer of Jabez* - enlarge my territory. Still nothing has happened. Why, you say? Doesn't God hear you? Doesn't God answer prayers? Yes, God hears you, and yes, God answers prayers. Let's take a look at the big picture to see what could have possibly happened.

You give someone a $20 bill and ask them to go to the store and buy you **one** loaf of bread. You only want **one** loaf because you need the rest of your money for gas. They return with **six** loaves of bread, because they were on sale. You are upset.

Now, let's see how God sees this. He gives you a paycheck and ask you to give him **10%** back, in tithes. You give him an **offering**, because you had to buy this dress. Do you think God *might* be upset? Let's go back to the big picture.

It is the 4th time this person has taken **your** money and done something different than what you requested. You say to yourself, this is the fifth and last time I am going to ask this person to do something for me, **if** they don't do what I ask them to do. The fifth and last time!

You give this person a receipt and ask them to return a pair of shoes, while they are at the mall. The refund is $97.24. The person is shopping and runs short of money. They borrow $50 of your refund, without asking you. They won't be able to pay you back for 2 weeks. You are livid!

Let's check with God again. He has given you four paychecks (over 2 months) and a raise. You still have not found a way to give the 10% he has requested, of you. With your raise, your paycheck is now $4000. With the $4000, you have decided that $400 is too much to give the Pastor. But God gives you a fifth chance! He enables you to get a $4000 bonus, you were not expecting. You open your checkbook to record the deposit. God is sitting on the edge of his chair, waiting for you to write the $400 check for tithes *plus* a check for an offering, since this bonus was truly a supernatural blessing. Instead, you get online and book a trip to Jamaica, for you and a couple of friends. Do you think God is livid?

What did you just do to your inheritance? What is the cause and effect of your *not* doing the right thing? God answered your prayer and increased your finances. The purpose of enlarging your territory is to help to enlarge His kingdom, here on earth. Do you think he will enlarge *your territory* for *your benefit only?* Do you think God should continue to give, give and receive little to nothing, in return? Would you continue to give to someone and receive nothing, in return? Not even a "thank you".

The bankruptcy courts are filled with "spiritual Christians" who vowed to get their finances together. You begged and bargained with God, only to let the devil deceive you into doing the wrong thing, one more time. You made promises, that you did not keep, all the way to bankruptcy court. You squandered your inheritance, on material possessions, and gave up your spiritual fruitfulness.

We must recognize that we have a role to play in increasing our inheritance. In order to rule over many things, you must be found faithful with what you have. Once again, this is a principle which we have a knowledge and understanding concern. Are we doing whatever is necessary to bring forth the blessings of Abraham, our inheritance?

Your children should be able to call you "blessed". We greet people with "I'm blessed", because of our Father. Are your children or your children's children able to greet people with "I'm blessed", because of the blessings that flow down, from you?

Proverbs 22:6 (KJV): "Train up a child in the way he should go: and when he is old, he will not depart for it".

CHILDREN AND MONEY

Train a child! Train a child! Train a child!

It is our responsibility, as parents, to teach our children how to handle money. The best training for our children is for them to develop and implement good money management skills early in life. To teach them how to manage money according to biblical guidelines, you, the parent, must first learn how to apply the biblical principles of finances, in your own life. The teaching needs to start early, in your child's life.

Parents must realize that their attitudes and ways of spending money greatly influence children. By being good examples in the way we handle money, our children will become good stewards over the resources with which they are entrusted. Therefore, it is necessary for you, as parents, to give your children a good model to emulate.

When I graduated from college, with 15 maxed out credit cards and over $100,000 in debt, I was not a good model for my son to follow. I was not operating within God's financial plan. As a matter of fact, I wasn't operating with any sort of plan. To narrow it all the way down, I wasn't operating at all. I was barely existing. My annual income was $25,000, and my debt was over $100,000 (and that didn't include a mortgage). This is why it was very important, for me, to get my finances together.

It was and is very important to me, to be a role model, for my son, in more ways than one. Finances has always been at the top of the list, especially with a son. The Bible says the man should be the head of his household. Where would the Christian family be if the head of each household had no financial control? There would a ton of confusion, divorce, strife, and no leadership within the family. Men, don't get into an ego trip and destroy your family over the checkbook. If your wife is better at handling the family's finances, then yield to her gift.

How do we instill this in our children? Parents must give them advice and guidance, starting at a very young age. We must begin to teach our children as soon as they start to handle money. When we give our children an allowance, we must teach them that 10% should be given as tithes on Sundays. When a child receives a gift of money for his birthday, Christmas, graduation, or any special occasion, we must teach our children to honor God with 10%.

I never gave my son in allowance because I did not believe in paying, for his learning to be responsible. However, for those special occasions where he received monies, he was taught to give 10% in tithes. He was, also, instructed to put 10% into a savings account for his "big" purchases, such as a bike, video game, etc.. When he reached adolescence, I took him to volunteer at a local church, for Christmas and Thanksgiving. I wanted him to see that there were people who were not as fortunate. More importantly, I wanted him to understand that God had blessed him, so that he could be a blessing to someone else, especially those in need. I considered this to be a very good financial lesson, because he learned to be grateful for what he had received. It was a picture of giving he was able to see, along with participating in the act of giving. I have found that a child understands the impact of giving better, when he actually participates or contributes, in some way, in helping the needy. It is, also, a good time for them to understand that giving is not always financially. Giving of their time and talent is just as worthy, and sometimes more appreciated.

When he started working, he opened a checking account, with the understanding the account would be used to make purchases and pay bills. At that time he had no bills, so I put money into his account to pay our utilities. For six months, he paid the utilities for our household. I used this great opportunity to teach him about waste--with utility companies, waste cost (Help me parents !).

As an adult, if he ever needed money, for something (such as car repair, not a new stereo system), I would make him a loan. I didn't charge him interest, and I let him pay me according to his pay, which varied. He always paid me back, in a timely manner. I didn't worry about him not paying me back, because he had been taught to pay his debts (along with my don't make momma "mad" reputation).

I have heard so many horror stories of parents loaning money to the adult children, and never receiving the money back. Many parents never received the money back, because of what they had taught their adult children about money, from their childhood. Sometimes we have to stop and think if this is simply payback for money we didn't payback to someone.

I've heard a lot of Christians say they are offended by the money sermons given by ministers. If you have a problem with the sermons the ministers are delivering, then have your own "money" Bible study at home, with your family and children. Research the Bible yourself and find out what the Bible says about finances, for you and your family. If you have adult children, invite them over and have a family Bible study, about finances. If you have younger children, then have the Bible study with them. They need to understand what the Bible says about finances. And it's best it comes from their role model, you, the parent.

Remember, just like ministers, we are responsible for what we teach our flock. In this case, our flock is our children. So stop and ask yourself, what am I teaching my children about finances through my actions, through my spending, through not paying my bills, through having bill collectors call the house (all hours of the evening), through having disconnection and eviction notices posted on the front door, and through having the children answer the phone saying "she's not home"?

Again, what are you teaching your children about finances? Is it sound, biblical, financial principles? Is it an honor to God? Will it make your children good financial stewards? Is it a projection of you as a good financial role model? I can't ask this enough, what are you teaching God's children about finances?

It is hard for young people, in particular, to be patient. They want and expect instant gratification, which is usually taught to them by their parents. We must teach them to be content with what they have been blessed to receive. We will discuss "contentment" more, in another chapter.

In an attempt to get your finances together, start a budget. If you have a family, it should be considered the "family" budget. Your children or anyone who receive benefits from your family finances should be included when you do the budget. Have everyone sit down and consider their comments and questions in your planning. Kids need to understand money does **not** grow on trees.

To begin, explain that a budget is merely directing your money where *you* want it to go rather than wondering where it went. Once they get a clear understanding of how money is handled, through a budget, they will have more respect for money and the things they ask to receive.

Proverbs 13:11 (KJV): "Wealth gotten by vanity shall be diminished: but he that gathered by labour shall increase".

THE CHURCH AND MONEY

Integrity matters!

Most books on the biblical principles of finances are written be ministers. Therefore, they don't deal with ministers and finances. Since I am not a minister, I feel we need to discuss the church's finances, from another prospective.

You need to know that how the money is handled in the church, flows down to you, because you are under that church's covering. If the minister is a leader who believes the monies of the church should be handled according to godly principles, financial blessings will flow downward to the congregation. If the minister handles the money in a selfish way, it blocks the flow of financial blessings, for the congregation.

The #1 ungodly financial principle that ministers commit is controlling the money. Many ministers think they must control the money in order to have control of the church. When in actuality, controlling the money is the "downfall" of the church. Why? It goes against the law of the land and the law of Godly principles. This is especially true in a new or small church.

Many ministers will probably burn this book for this statement--**A minister should not handle or touch the money.** All monies should be handled by the Treasurer and/or the Finance Committee. The church's bylaws clearly (or they should) define the role of the Treasurer, as the person who **handles the finances**. None of the bylaws say, "Don't touch the money. Give it to the minister." Nor do they say, "The minister must be in control of all financial matters". The minister is called for God's purpose-the spiritual leader.

On that same note, if you are a Treasurer, in a church, and never handle or see the money after it is collected on Sunday, then you need to resign from your position. All finances of the church are governed by the IRS. If there is ever a discrepancy with the finances, you are the responsible party and could possibly, be held liable, financially and legally for any wrongdoing.

Here is how the flow of money should go:

> The money should be collected and taken directly to the finance department (or counting room). The money should be counted by Trustees plus the Treasurer. The next day, the money should be deposited in the bank. All bills should be paid by the appointed person. (I am saying appointed person, because there are so many different titles.) The appointed person is usually the Church Secretary or the Business Manager. The number of people involved in this process depends on the size of the church and the size of the offering. Annually, there should be an audit of the church's books, by an outside individual or firm.

Another key point: The success of a church will depend, largely, on the minister doing was God has ordained him to do and allow the

Trustees (Board Members) to handle the day-to-day operations. The church is a place of worship, but is, also, a business. And it should operate, as such. In all successful churches, the minister is the CEO (or President) of the corporation and attend the least amount of meetings, as possible. The most important meeting for the minister, to attend, is the annual meeting. At this meeting, the minister informs the members of the vision for the church, **according to what God has revealed to him**. Some ministers will announce that it is God's vision for the church, when it is really their personal agenda. So, as members of the Board, it is your duty to consult with God (in prayer and fasting) before making decisions. Remember the minister is not the only person with God on speed-dial.

It is vital that the church stay focus on God's will for the church. Success and growth will be inedible, if you just trust in God. It is vital for new and small church pastors and leaders to attend at least one Pastor and Leadership Conference, at a very successful church, to learn how to operate their church, according to God's will.

The #2 ungodly financial principle committed in the church is leaders or members that knowingly participate in the Pastor's wrongdoing. The word **loyalty** rings in my ear. Here are some of the statements that I have heard:

> "I must be a loyal servant."

> "I am loyal to my Pastor."

> "The Pastor means well."

> "He's going to get it together."

> "I'm just doing what the Lord told me to do."

> "No one else would help the Pastor."

> "He is just doing what the Lord told him to do."

> "He's royalty, so he must know what he is doing."

These are some of the most lame excuses I have ever heard.

Here is my question to you--If someone asked you to steal some money from a sick, elderly person, would you be a willing participant? If you decided to participate, would you use any of the excuses above, as to why you assisted this person?

Well, if a sick, elderly person paid their tithes to your church, from their Social Security check, which is so low below the poverty line it can't be found, and you know the minister is in control of the money and not handling it in a godly manner, did you just collaborate with the minister in stealing from the elderly? Yes, you did. Not directly, but indirectly. That's like saying, you were with the person that robbed the bank, but you shouldn't be prosecuted, because you didn't get any money.

If you speak out, will you be slaughtered by the church? Yes, but do the right thing. Speak out! Don't just resign or move your membership and hide behind the caller ID, out of shame. Let it be known. If the Trustees don't agree, then move on. Don't participate in the work of the devil. Remove you and your family from under that covering. Go to a church where financial blessings are flowing, because the minister is making sure the money is handled in a godly manner. There is a lot of mess going on in the church, by messy people. Don't make any decisions based on gossip. Ask God for a revelation, if there is some doubt. Don't act on gossip, know the facts.

Personally, myself, I like churches that post the finances in the church bulletin. It eliminates a lot of unbelief. Our unbelief prevents God from doing mighty works in our lives. Plus, what message are we sending to the world when the Church can't pay its bills? What message are we sending to the world when the pastor preaches about a God that supply all of our needs, yet the pastor is begging every Sunday? What message are we sending to the world when the Church is more interested in adorning its building than in sharing what they have, to reach the lost? What message are we sending to the world when the Pastor's preaching is not what he really believes, through his actions?

It is not my intention to slander the ministers nor the church, but the church is ran by humans, and humans are subject to error and sin. Money is a big temptation! It will change the best of us. Over the years, I have seen it destroy churches. Most of the time, it is the greed of the pastor. However, there have been many incidents where people in leadership have stolen from the church. Just pray and ask God to send you to a church where the covering is blessed.

Hebrews 13:5 (KJV): "Let your conversation be without covetousness; and be content with such things as ye have for he hath said, I will never leave thee, nor forsake thee".

GREED VS CONTENTMENT

Greedy living is simply--living our lives with our affection on obtaining more worldly goods. Christians often ask God to meet their desires or lusts. We feel like we can provide our needs. We just need a little help with the extras. We ask God to give us things that would serve no purpose other than to feed our greed.

If your desire is for the riches of this world rather than the riches of Christ, you will fall into temptation, which is nothing more than a trap. And through this trap, the Bible says that "many have wandered away from the faith". In Deuteronomy 8, Moses warned the people of Israel concerning their greed and forgetting what God had done for them.

Fawning over riches and possessions can make one forget about God altogether. There is nothing more dangerous than that. And a life that does not take God into consideration is a life that will be full of pain and empty in purpose.

There are many examples, in the Bible, of how painful money can be when we are not content, disciplined and in control of it, but how it controls us. It is here that we must be very careful, for the lure of money, can take us down some horrible and destructive roads.

Job is a perfect example of what it means to be content. Job was a very rich man, yet he lost everything. Everything! Yet, he did not commit suicide or lose his mind. Why? Because he trusted God, and his contentment was in God. Many of you would have committed suicide or lost your mind. Why? Because we worship "things", and our contentment is in riches and possessions.

To be content, we must have knowledge of the

Principle of Contentment. Contentment is knowing God's plan for your life and being peaceful about it, whether we have much or little. Read I Timothy 6 to get an understanding of what we can lose through greed and what we can gain through contentment.

Greed is a path of destruction, with the devil as the tour guide. Many of us are walking down that path, right now. We feel that "if only" we could climb that corporate ladder, take home a high six figure paycheck, and have our name on a corner office, we will be happy and content. Our minds are full of "if only" dreams. Without God in our life, all of these things will be short-lived and with chaos.

It goes without saying that we need money to live and meet the basic needs we have, but why do we have a desire to have more money? We have the desire to have more money because we expect it to enhance our lives. To a degree, all these needs can be met on the surface, but the results is temporary. True satisfaction can only come from God.

Many of you may be thinking now, or have thought in the past, as many people do, "If I had enough money, I could do what I want it do, and then I would be happy!" John D.

Rockefeller, the richest man of his day and first billionaire, could certainly have bought any pleasures he wanted, but he knew that true satisfaction takes more than possessions and leisure time. Look at how many billions of dollars Warren Buffett has just given away. Look at the hundreds of millions of dollar Oprah Winfrey has given away. It appears their satisfaction and pleasure is in giving and not receiving. They have what I call a "super, abundant, willingness to give". They take II Corinthians 9:6-7 to the next level. In essence, it says you reap what you sow.

Please remember the primary problem with finding your identity in money is that significance does not come from being worth something. Significance comes from being worth something to somebody. If your child is terminally ill, the amount of money in your bank account is not important to the child. What is important (or significant) to your child, is that you are by his side and praying on his behalf. No amount of money can keep God from declaring, "Your child's life is over, now!" Unfortunately, it takes drastic incidents, such as death, for many of us to realize the real worth of money. Worst of all, riches cannot provide any security whatsoever in eternity. All the riches in the world are not enough to buy your way into heaven when you die.

Money only gives you a cheaper kind of identity. If you have more money than others, people may respect you for it, but that by itself doesn't make you worth anything to them. And if you ever quit making (or having) money, you would lose people's respect, and with it, you will also lose all the identity you derived from their respect.

Practice the Principle of Contentment. Know God's plan for your life and being peaceful about it. When God is our joy, our delight, our contentment, no one can touch that. When our joy, our delight, our contentment is in riches and possessions, then our joy goes up and down. That's no way to live, so we must learn to be content.

Write this down and put it some place where you can see it on a daily basis.

Godliness+contentment=great gain

Proverbs 21: 5 (KJV): "The thoughts of the diligent tend only to plenteousness; but of every one that is hasty only to want".

GOD'S PLAN

What is God's plan for your finances? Do you
know? Do you consult with God concerning
your finances, **before** you start to spend? Or
do you wait until you are broke, busted, and
disgusted, and cry to God for help. If you knew
and understood God's plan for your finances,
then your life and that of your family would be
more prosperous.

God wants to raise up individuals **within the
body of Christ** who can be trusted with money.
I added "within the body of Christ", because the
world is better stewards with their money than
Christians. He wants **us** to get our financial

houses in order, not only to meet our needs, but, also, so we will be able to reach out to those around us. He wants us to be in a position to give so that His covenant might be established on earth. This will never happen in our lives unless we learn how to become good stewards over the money that have been entrusted to our care.

God has outlined principles in the Bible that teaches us how to overcome our financial struggles. As I stated earlier in the book, we are not lacking knowledge. We know exactly what to do, however, we fail to do the right thing, because we are more concerned about self. For that reason, this will be the longest chapter of this book. For the Bible says in all your getting, get an understanding. So this chapter will be dedicated to your understanding God's financial system and God's plan for your finances.

The Bible is the number one source for understanding God's financial plan. God's financial plan is not complicated. It is a very basic plan. Proverbs 24:3 (KJV) states, "Through wisdom is an house builded; and by understanding it is established". Wisdom builds. We must make a commitment to learn his word, and be willing to take action on his word. We must read the Bible to give us long-term solutions to our financial problems and not quick fixes. To completely understand God's plan for our finances, we must first understand the 4 Spirits of God financial plan.

The four Spirits of God's Financial Plan are..
1. Spirit of Poverty
2. Spirit of Expectancy
3. Spirit of Wealth
4. Spirit of Giving

We will discuss each one individually, note how each apply to our lives, and how to overcome or implement the Spirit into our daily rituals.

SPIRIT OF POVERTY

What is the Spirit of Poverty? It is simply lack. It is the lack of money, lack of knowledge, lack of planning, lack of giving, lack of discipline, lack of commitment, lack of consistency, lack of what you need, lack of understanding money, lack of organization, and the lack of understanding God's financial plan.

You can set yourself free from the Spirit of Poverty, by changing your mindset. Many of us have grown-up with a poverty mindset. How many of you have had these teachings in church?

- Money is the root of all evil
- To be poor, means you are humble
- It is a generational curse
- It's OK to be young and in debt
- You're going to be broke, just like your parents

And the list could go on and on. It is important that *you* get an understanding of God's word and not just take it from the pulpit. I love it when Dr. Creflo Dollar tells his congregation to *not* take his word, but find out for themselves. It is *you* (and not the Pastor) who is responsible for the money God had entrusted with you. Let's find out how to set yourself "free" and break the Spirit of Poverty.

5 WAYS TO BREAK THE SPIRIT OF POVERTY

1. Prayer--Ask God
2. Surplus--What should you do with it
3. Debt Reduction--Stop with the credit cards
4. Saving Plan--Increase your saving plan
5. Start Giving--Give to be a blessing

PRAYER

Now, let's support this with scripture. Matthew 7:7 (KJV) says, "Ask and it shall be given". Ask how--through prayer.

In 1985, little did I know that my debt was headed to over $100,000. My son was born premature. The doctors told me he would only live for 24 hours. He was born on a Monday morning, and by Thursday he was still alive, but only by the grace of God. At that time, I sat in my hospital bed and prayed a prayer to God, asking him to change my financial situation. One of the first things I did, was to admit that I had made many mistakes and that I had gotten *myself* into this financial mess. I was ready to change my financial situation. It was at that time, that God stepped in and began to turn my finances completely around.

I know that God answers prayers. You should take this time, right now, to pray a heartfelt prayer to God and ask him to change your financial situation. You must be willing to change your habits (as I did), be committed to becoming a better steward, and practice daily discipline. God needs you to do your part.

SURPLUS

In Proverbs 6, consider the work of the ant! We must learn to look at our wastefulness and learn how to spend only what we earn. We must, also, learn how to cut *out* and not just cut *down*, in some cases. We must start creating a surplus. Once we have a surplus, which is more than enough, we must have godly knowledge of what to do with the surplus. Should we go shopping, should we bless someone else with 100% of it or some of it, or should we save it?

DEBT REDUCTION

Proverbs 22:7 (KJV): "The rich rules over the poor; the borrower is a servant to the lender".

What is debt? According to the thesaurus the synonyms for debt are: to owe, to be obligated, in deficit, in default, in solvent, in over one's head, in arrears, destitute, penniless, needy, distressed, living hand to mouth, hard up, beaten down, unable to make ends meet, embarrassed, broke, busted. I think you should read each of these again and I want you to read them slowly and see which one(s) apply to you.

Debt is a thief. It is of the world, causes worry and anxiety, causes conflict and illnesses, takes your focus off of God, causes you to live from the day before payday to payday, stops us for being a blessing to others, and causes us to sin. We know what God says about debt, through our previous knowledge. God says we should be the lender and not the borrower.

Statistics shows that the more educated you are, the more you shop. It, also, shows that the more educated you are, the more debt you have from impulsive shopping. Final conclusion, educated people finances are worse than the un or undereducated person. Why is this so? Because the more money we make, the more materialistic, selfish, and greedy we become. Proverbs 21: 20 (KJV) states that a foolish (or stupid) man spends his money as fast as he gets it. Before we know it, we have created massive amounts of debt.

SAVING PLAN

God is a God of planning and organization. Therefore, if you fail to plan, you can plan to fail. You must plan. Planning ahead is essential if you are going to be a good steward and a good saver.

The scripture says "Write the vision and make it plain on tables", Habakkuk 2:2 (KJV). Make your goals and plans plain. "Where there is no vision, the people perish", Proverbs 29:18 (KJV). No money in the bank shows a lack of planning and goal setting. Show God that you can plan and organize your finances and begin to reap the blessings.

START GIVING

Acts 20:35 (KJV):   "More blessed to give than to receive".

Proverbs 11:24 (KJV):   "The generous man will be prosperous".

Malachi 3:10 (KJV): "Bring ye all of the tithes into the storehouse".

We know these scriptures. We have repeated these scriptures, over and over again. The scriptures on giving could go on and on, but what about the most valuable gift God gave us--His Son. He gave His only son, for our sake. Yet, we still are not faithful givers. Become committed to God's financial plan and break the Spirit of Poverty.

SPIRIT OF EXPECTANCY

The Spirit of Expectancy is simply "expectations". It is what we expect, from whom, and why we expect something. Do we expect more, expect the best, expect to be blessed, expect to have favor, or expect God to show up?

The most powerful sermon I have heard was delivered by award-winning gospel singer Rev Jesse Dixon. It was entitled "The Spirit of Expectancy". Through this message, I realized I was not expecting any great things. I was simply taking what life was dealing me. It was not until I applied the Spirit of Expectancy to my life, did I began to experience the "best". I began to **expect** the best, **expect** more, **expect** to be blessed, **expect** to have favor, and **expect** God to show-up and show-out.

For many, your expectations are the worst. You expect your daughter to be an unwed mother. You expect your son to be incarcerated. You expect poor economic situations to determine your future. You don't expect anything beyond your faith, which is usually smaller than the mustard seed.

Many Christians expect the church to take care of them. They always have a sad situation that requires someone to give them something. You know who I am talking about. It is that "saint" you dread speaking to, because you know they were looking for someone to tell their sad, sad story of destitute. I have to ask of that "saint", you are expecting God to give to you, but who are you giving to? To be Christ-like, you have to be a giver. Mostly you have to be a giver of *something that means something to you.*

Saints, can God use you to be an instrument for repairing broken dreams? Can God have a Spirit of Expectancy in you? Can God expect the best from you? Can God expect you to be a blessing to others? Can God expect a Spirit of Excellence in all things, from you? Can God expect you to be a testimony of his goodness? If not, why not? You expect all of these things and some more of God.

Let see what God's word says about the Spirit of Expectancy and see if you are in line with His word. First, we must understand that we have a covenant with God and know the covenant agreement. In Genesis 12:2, the covenant agreement states that God will bless you and expect you to be a blessing to others.

Giving or being a blessing to others is God's way for us to tap into His supernatural blessings.

Deuteronomy 28 says you can <u>expect</u> to be blessed in your going and your coming; in the field and in the city. By the same token, God <u>expects</u> you to be a blessing. That's his Spirit of Expectancy--he gives, you gives!

Our actions and our words will get the Cycle of Expectancy started. By our actions, I mean, doing what God <u>expects</u> us to do. Through words, you should speak daily confirmations of God's promises to the children of his kingdom. As Rev. Jesse Dixon spoke in his message-- <u>expect</u> to be blessed.

SPIRIT OF WEALTH

Now that we are expecting to be blessed, let's find out what to do with all of the wealth we are about to receive.

What is the Spirit of Wealth? It is living wealthy where you are *now*. It is being *thankful* and *grateful* for what you have. It is knowing that you can't move to the next level of wealth without knowledge.

Hosea 4:6 (KJV): "My people are destroyed for lack of knowledge because thou hast rejected knowledge". As I have stated numerous times before, we have the knowledge but don't use the knowledge we have acquired. Knowledge= money. Without knowledge, we will continue to live in financial decay. Without using our knowledge, we will have broken homes, broken dreams, and broken lives. Our economic circumstances will continue to be beyond our control and lack will control our daily lives. We will live under the curse of the Spirit of Poverty.

Many of us, today, are struggling to pay for student loans for bachelor's, master's and doctorate's degrees to acquire money, in the world. God's knowledge is merely the cost of a Bible. It is cheaper than a college textbook. It is given to us "free" on Sunday. Still, we live under the curse of the Spirit of Poverty and lack the necessary funds to be a blessing.

The church is the most vital part of educating God's people about God's financial plan. It has a responsibility to teach God's financial system. Yet, many pastors blast the teaching of "money". Some pastors blast the teaching for a lack of knowledge, on their part. Some blast it for a lack of understanding. This is why it is important that you get an understanding for yourself (remember Dr. Creflo Dollar!).

I have to ask the question-did these pastors not understand they were using the financial system they were blasting, every Sunday? Reciting Malachi 3:10 before the offering, selling chicken dinners for the building fund, asking for donations to help the needy, and praying for money to support their families and the church families are all part of a financial system. They were not necessarily part of God's financial system, but they dealt with finances. They seem to blast the teaching but not the asking.

If your pastor does not teach God's financial system, remember this is a covering you are under and it affects your finances, too. It could be creating lack in your life, in more ways than one. And if pastors don't change their thinking and seek knowledge, about finances and financing God's kingdom, their churches will continue to be covered with a Spirit of Poverty. Their members will be in financial bondage.

Be Good To God's Money

II Corinthians 8:9 proves that Christ <u>became</u> poor so that we can be rich. <u>Became</u> poor-- does that mean he was rich <u>before</u>? Does that mean it is OK to be <u>rich</u>? For so many years, we were told it was a sin to seek riches. Not only is it OK to be rich, but it is a tremendous blessing to transfer wealth to others. Christ transferred his wealth to us; therefore, he <u>expects</u> us to transfer wealth to others.

Growing up in Mississippi, I did not hear teachings on finances. As a matter of fact, I did not hear any teachings on tithing. Most of those same churches I attended as a kid are still the same. The same building, the same location, the same attendance, and the same preaching. Many of the churches have different ministers, but the message, apparently, has not changed.

I believe God wants to raise up individuals within the body of Christ who can be trusted with money. He wants us to get our financial houses in order, so we can be a blessing to others and establish His covenant on this earth. This will never happen until we learn to be good stewards over our money. God knows who he can trust. Many of you are not faithful with the money you already have, yet you continue to ask for more. Due to your lack of discipline, God knows he can not trust you with large amounts of money. The better you manage the money with which you have been entrusted, the more money you will have to manage.

To those Christians, who are willing to pay the price to learn how to handle money according to God's financial system, God will give you supernatural abilities to receive financial prosperity. God wants you to have money. He wants to restore your family. He wants to repair broken dreams. He wants to break the Spirit of Poverty. However, you must be willing to accept the responsibility, as stewards, of how you handle money, if you are going to walk in God's supernatural blessings.

Deuteronomy 28:2 (KJV) states, "And all these blessings shall come on thee and overtake thee, if thou shalt hearken unto the voice of the Lord thy God". Deuteronomy 8:17-18 (KJV), "And thou say in thine heart, My power and the might of *mine* hand hath gotten me this wealth. But thou shalt remember the Lord thy God; for it is he that giveth thee power to get wealth, that he may establish his covenant which he sware unto thy fathers, as it is this day".

Phrased another way--God has given us the power to get wealth (if we are willing to work for it), but we must not forget Him. If God gave you $1million, today. Can he trust you to give him $100,000, first? You said "yes"? Before you declare "yes" as your final answer, think about the wish list you made, years ago, of what you would do if you got a million dollars. A house, furniture, and a Bentley can wipe out a million dollar. So, now, rethink your answer-- can God trust you?

The Spirit of Wealth overshadows the individuals who understand God's financial system. They are operating in the Spirit of Expectancy and the Spirit of Giving. That's why the rich keeps getting richer. And the poor are getting poorer, because they are operating in the Spirit of Poverty.

This is the part where many of us "block" our blessings. We are excellent receivers but poor givers. When we feel that we have 'arrived", we tend to forget how we got to where we are, today. Or we feel we don't "owe" anybody--I got mine; you better get yours. We like to feel we got there on our own. I have heard so many people say "nobody helped me to get where I am, today". Without knowing and knowing those individuals, I beg to differ with them. For I know, no one can make it alone. I can't even begin to count the number of times God has stepped into my life and taken control of some mess I had made or put the right people, in the right place, at the right time. So, stop blocking your blessings by being selfish. Change your mind, change your heart and become a cheerful giver. Learn to reap the financial rewards, according to God. Today is the day to reverse the curse.

SPIRIT OF GIVING

The Spirit of Giving is a condition of the heart that shows thanksgiving. To possess the Spirit of Giving, you must be a compassionate giver, cheerful giver, and not a giver out of greed. If you possess the Spirit of Expectancy, God will multiply your seed, to possess the Spirit of Giving.

Dr. Robert Schuller made a profound statement--"The joy of giving is the crowning purpose of living". Giving above and beyond what is required of you, is a profound statement you can make.

Am I a cheerful giver? Do I give with the right attitude? Do I give out of greed? Or do I give from the heart? God is looking for individuals who have honesty and integrity of the heart to trust with the true riches.   When I think of a person He has trusted with the true riches, I think of Oprah. She has always had a "true" joy in giving to others, even when she didn't make a lot of money. My greatest admiration, for her, is her humbleness, even as a billionaire. Can you be humble, with much? Can God trust you?

If your finances could talk, what would they say? If your finances could go to church and gossip (like we do), what secrets would they tell? If a report could be issued, in church would the final numbers be in red or black? If we could talk to your checkbook, wallet, or bank account, what would they scream? If someone arrived at your finance department, would the sign say, "Closed, due to embarrassment"?

One thing, for sure, they will definitely tell who you really worship. They will tell the congregation whether or not you worship the mall or God's kingdom. They will tell whether or not you are thankful or ungrateful. They will tell whether or not you trust God or your next refinance. They will tell your *true* Lord.

If we put our focus on giving, when our money talks it won't embarrass us, with what it has to say. In today society, money don't talk anymore. It just quietly slips away, because we have not committed our finances to God.

There is no way to grow to spiritual maturity without committing your finances to the Lord. We can serve God, or we can serve money. We can't serve both. It is spiritually immature to try to serve both. He can't have our hearts without our money. The Bible says...where your treasure is...there will your heart be also.

Our checkbook, wallet, and bank account should show that God is the head of our lives, not money. It should show that we are wise investors. We invest in things that last, not things that don't. It should show that we are investing in the Kingdom. It should speak volumes as to how much we *trust* God. When we refuse to give our tithes to the church, we are saying that we don't trust God to do what He said He would do. It should show how thankful we are for all God has done for us. And giving of our time, talents, and money provides us a way to show God how very thankful we are for His sacrifice, on our behalf.

God has given us so much, therefore we should have a super abundant willingness to give. And just like we balance our checkbook, (yes, there are people, like myself, that balance their checkbook) we must balance our receiving with our giving.

Take out your checkbook, wallet, and bank statement. Put them to your ears and listen. What are they saying about you and your finances? Are they telling a story that pleasing to God? You must be honest with yourself, about what you are hearing, because it will be your blessings that will flow away. Just like you reap what you sow, someone else will reap what will flow.

In ending, I would like to suggest to everyone to read the entire book of Proverbs. I have always looked at the book of Proverbs, as "The Guidebook of Life". If your finances are not together, then is a great chance that your life is not together. This is the book to read to put the pieces of your life back together, which in turn will put your finances on track.

I truly hope that if you have read this far into this book, that you are sincere about gaining supernatural wealth, in your life. If so, start with a prayer and begin to take action. I will share with you the prayer I prayed, that changed my life and my finances.

Dear God,
I am in a mess again! Please help me find the answers to my financial problems. I need your guidance to show me how to get out of this mess. Please lead me and guide down the right paths, for I have taken a wrong turn somewhere. Please enable me to see the opportunities you present to relieve this burden. And give me the courage and knowledge to take advantage of the doors you open for me. Thank you for the lessons I will learn from my mistakes. And thank you for the answers to this temporary situation. Amen

ABOUT THE AUTHOR

Lisa Frye is the bestselling author of the highly-acclaimed *National* Bestseller, <u>Be Good To Your Money</u> and publisher of the "award-winning" *Be Good To Your Money* newsletter.

Her invaluable advice has been featured in *Woman's World Magazine, Roosevelt Review, Nevada Woman, Gospel Truth Magazine,* and newspapers across the country.

She has been featured on ABC, CBS, NBC, WGN, WORD Network, and BET, in print media and on radio waves across the nation. She can be heard monthly, on WYLD/FM 98 in New Orleans, LA.

She, currently, resides in Southern Nevada with her son, Quintin.

To schedule a FREE *Be Good To Your Money* seminar for your church or organization, please visit Lisa's website at:

www.LisaFrye.com

Or call: 866-750-0188